Goldilocks and the Three Bears

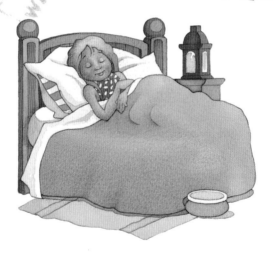

Barrie Wade and Kristina Stephenson

W
FRANKLIN WATTS
LONDON • SYDNEY

Once upon a time there were three
bears – Mummy Bear, Daddy Bear and
Baby Bear. They all lived in a cottage
near the woods.

One morning, Mummy Bear made porridge, but it was really hot.
"Let's go for a walk and let our porridge cool down," said Mummy Bear.
So they did.

At the same time, a little girl called
Goldilocks was out walking too. She
noticed the three bears' cottage and
walked up the path.

Goldilocks didn't even knock on the door. She crept inside and soon found the three bowls of porridge that the bears had left to cool.

"I'm hungry," she said.

First she tasted Daddy Bear's porridge,

but it was much too hot.

Next she tried Mummy Bear's porridge,
but it was much too cold.

Then she ate a spoonful of Baby Bear's porridge. Baby Bear's porridge was just right and Goldilocks ate it all up! "Yum, yum. Delicious!" she said.

Goldilocks had eaten the porridge
too quickly and now she felt full.
"I want a rest," she said.
She noticed three chairs. Daddy Bear's
chair was much too hard.

Mummy Bear's chair was too soft and she could not get comfortable.

Baby Bear's chair was just right, but Goldilocks was too big for the little, wooden chair.

When she sat down on it,

the chair broke.

Now Goldilocks felt tired,

so she went upstairs.

"I need a sleep," she said.

First of all she sat on Daddy Bear's bed, but it was much too hard.

Next she tried Mummy Bear's bed, but it was much too soft. She could not lie down properly.

Then she climbed into Baby Bear's bed.

Baby Bear's bed was just right.

"It's so comfortable!" said Goldilocks.

She lay down and fell fast asleep.

Soon the three bears came back from their walk.

"I'm ready for my breakfast," said Baby Bear.

"Someone's been eating my porridge," growled Daddy Bear. "What's happening here?"

18

"Someone's been eating my porridge as well," said Mummy Bear.

"Look! Someone's been eating my porridge," cried Baby Bear, "and they've eaten it all up."

"Someone's been sitting in my chair," growled Daddy Bear. "What is going on?"

"Someone's been sitting in my chair as well," said Mummy Bear.

"Look! Someone's been sitting in my
chair," cried Baby Bear, "and they've
broken it."

"Let's look around," growled Daddy Bear. So the three bears went upstairs.

"Someone's been sleeping in my bed," growled Daddy Bear, "and they have left it untidy."

"Someone's been sleeping in my bed as well," said Mummy Bear. "They have left it untidy too."

"Someone's been sleeping in my bed,"
cried Baby Bear. "Look! It's a girl and
she's still there!"

Just then Goldilocks woke up, gave a little squeal, jumped out of the bed and ran away as fast as she could.

Baby Bear watched her go.

"I wish she had stayed," said Baby

Bear. "Then I would have someone

to play with."

About the story

Goldilocks and the Three Bears is a fairy tale that was first written down by Robert Southey in 1837. It was called "The Story of the Three Bears" and had an old woman instead of a little girl breaking into the bears' house. The bears were three different-sized male bears. Over time, the old woman became a little girl called Goldilocks, and the three bears became a family!

Be in the story!

Imagine you are Goldilocks. You must say sorry to Baby Bear for eating his porridge and breaking his chair.

Now imagine you are Baby Bear. What will you say to Goldilocks? Would you still like to play with her?

First published in 2014 by
Franklin Watts
338 Euston Road
London
NW1 3BH

Franklin Watts Australia
Level 17/207 Kent Street
Sydney
NSW 2000

The artwork for this story first appeared in
Leapfrog: Goldilocks and the Three Bears

ISBN 978 1 4451 2843 6 (hbk)
ISBN 978 1 4451 2844 3 (pbk)
ISBN 978 1 4451 2846 7 (library ebook)
ISBN 978 1 4451 2845 0 (ebook)

Series Editor: Jackie Hamley
Series Advisor: Catherine Glavina
Series Designer: Cathryn Gilbert

Printed in China

Franklin Watts is a divison of
Hachette Children's Books,
an Hachette UK company.
www.hachette.co.uk